Workers in My City

Sharon Coan

MW00917031

Publishing Credits

Rachelle Cracchiolo, M.S.Ed., *Publisher*
Conni Medina, M.A.Ed., *Managing Editor*
Jamey Acosta, *Content Director*
Dona Herweck Rice, *Series Developer*
Robin Erickson, *Multimedia Designer*

Image Credits: Cover, p.1 (front) ©Don Mason/Alamy, (back) ©iStock.com/Beau Meyer; pp.3, 12 ©iStock.com/Tony Tremblay; p.4 Blend Images/Don Mason/Getty Images; p.6 ©iStock.com/snapphoto; p.7 Holger Leue/Getty Images; p,8 ©iStock.com/Susan Chiang; p.9 ©Peter Horree/Alamy; p.11 ©iStock.com/Peter Macdiarmid; pp.10, 12, Back cover ©iStock.com/Steve Debenport; all other images from Shutterstock.

Teacher Created Materials

5301 Oceanus Drive
Huntington Beach, CA 92649-1030
http://www.tcmpub.com
ISBN 978-1-4938-2146-4
© 2016 Teacher Created Materials, Inc.

city

city worker

city worker

city worker

city worker

city worker

city worker

city worker

city worker

Words to Know

city

worker